8

Unbreakable Commandments For a High Conversion Website

Shark Bite Coaching

DEDICATION

This book is dedicated to entrepreneurs and business professionals who are ready to take their businesses to the next level.

I wish you luck in your success and hope that I can help even just a little bit.

CONTENTS

INTRODUCTION

The evolution of the Internet has introduced us to an age that mankind has never experienced before. Technology moves faster than ever, and keeps our creativity set on "super" active. Businesses and dreams can be made just by sitting down and turning on your computer or laptop. [Well, ok, you may actually have to click your mouse or hit a few keys...] The world of business and entrepreneurship is just waiting for you to dive in and take a bite, and one of the most important things you can do is to build your own company website to launch your virtual brand and manage your brand's online reputation [visit www.social-media-management-group.com/ORMR for assistance].

Why is having your own website necessary? Most people nowadays have their own accounts in Facebook, Twitter, Google + and more, and by having your own website, you immediately bring your business within reach of anyone who can surf the web or access the Internet. [Of course, combining your website and social media efforts can create even more exceptional results; this book focuses solely on your website. If you would like guidance or assistance on social media efforts, visit www.social-media-management-group.com. Another reason is that not everyone, even if they live in the same city as you, can easily pop into your store or office, but they CAN visit your website anytime they want to. Your virtual store is open 24 hours a day, 7 days a week, 365 ¼ days a year.

Very few people nowadays do not use the Internet on a regular basis (whether checking email, bidding on eBay, or reading breaking news—just to mention a few tasks that I do quite a bit of…), and having your own website means that your products and services are instantly more accessible to them. They can easily view all you have to offer in the comfort of their home or office (and if you have a mobile site or app—anywhere they can get a signal on their smartphone). With your company website, a simple picture and description of your products will often garner enough interest to engage your visitor in a purchase or, at least, a request for more information.

Your website needs to have a strategy to convert visitors and Internet traffic into leads; by turning your website into a lead generation tool, you are creating a high conversion website. You built your website to earn money, and you've probably heard it said that the money is in the list…so the more conversions you have (through a sale, request for information, subscription to a newsletter, registration for a free report, et. al.) the bigger the list you will be able to direct your highly-targeted offers to. For a website to have high conversion, it needs to be adaptive and meet the needs of your potential customers. Adaptive web design and conversion rate optimization are just two more buzz words for processes that have grown out of the necessity of the economy and the market today. They are also a response to the availability of evolving technologies, and there may be aspects of them both that you may be interested in or find very useful. We will look at these topics in subsequent books as they will require a much more in-depth and technical writing approach. This book is meant to be a quick read with some useful tips that you can implement immediately to improve your existing website or to get your new website up and running as quickly as possible while still fulfilling its ultimate role of a business lead generator and sales closer.

The Internet is also one of the best marketing tools available today and having your own website means you can maintain a virtual relationship with your customer [which for most people is as good as or better than a "real" face-to-face relationship] and even capture new ones. You can also stay updated on the latest trends in the business and marketing arena, ensuring that your company stays on top of the game. [Visit http://bit.ly/Z7Kuhd for a Free Report on five great tools to monitor your customers, competitors, and web trends].

Now that you know how important it is to have your own website and virtual brand, it's now time to read on and uncover the eight unbreakable commandments for a high conversion business website.

COMMANDMENT #1
YOUR WEBSITE SHALL NOT
STAND ALONE

Synchronize and update your website along with your marketing and business plans—on a regular basis...

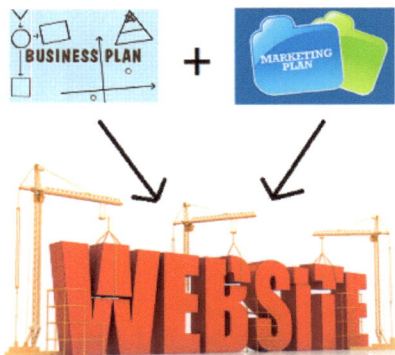

As an entrepreneur you are already familiar with how important a business plan is to your company and the growth of your company, and planning for your website should be done the same way. Your business plan details your goals and basic ideas for how you will achieve them, and your website should be a part of that effort as well as offering an outlet to prove your expertise. This means that your website shouldn't just be used for selling your products and services but also serve as a good base of information for everything anyone may want to know about your company, your products, or the problems you can help them solve.

Your website should be one of the most important aspects of your marketing efforts, and this means that it should also reflect the newest trends in your marketing strategies and up-to-date information on your <u>industry's</u> issues and successes (not just your company's).

If you are offering discounts and limited deals, your website can provide this information in real time. Your company's plans to improve, remove, and re-price products and services should also be updated on your website. The content of your website should be accurate, straight-forward, and customer focused, so remember to update it as often as you do your business and marketing plans (if not more often).

There are times when you may want to adjust prices or offer discounts or samples, and this means updating your website in a timely fashion to fit the promotions and trends that your small business is offering at the present. When you properly monitor the results of your website sales and analytics of the site traffic driven by your distinct marketing campaigns, you will realize the importance of keeping it up to date. The last thing you want is people contacting you about sales or free service trials that are no longer available. How Embarrassing…

Regular updates will also help keep your website among the top search engine rankings. When most people search for a product or service through a search engine like Google, they rarely, if ever, click past the first page to additional results. If their answers are not evident on the first page, they will search again using different keywords or phrases. When your website content becomes out of date (which happens very quickly in today's business environment), your website will quickly lose its page ranking as fewer people visit it, and fewer relevant keywords (which are constantly churning) will be represented.

Keep your website up-to-date, informative, and even entertaining, and you will also make it fun to visit, and easy to find.

TIP: The tone and messaging of your website should be in line with your company's value proposition, and it should also show the latest trends and strategies detailed in your marketing plan. Check that your website is working correctly every day, and schedule updates once a week (at a minimum).

COMMANDMENT #2
THOU SHALL NOT OVERWHELM YOUR POTENTIAL CUSTOMERS WITH TOO MUCH INFORMATION OR TOO MANY PRODUCTS

Decide what core products and key services your website should focus on

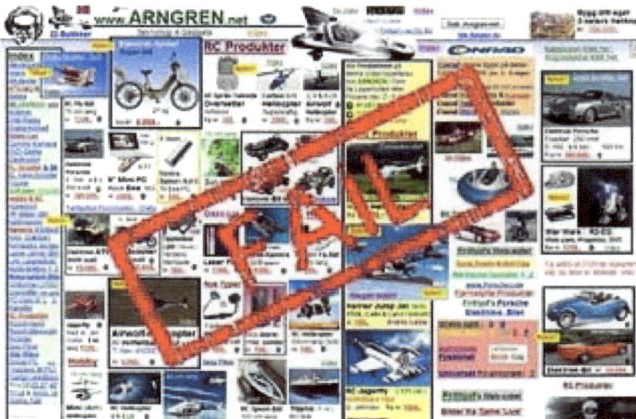

You are not Amazon and probably won't be able to sell all your products and services through your website, so focus on the ones that can be readily understood, priced more generously, and efficiently delivered. However, this doesn't mean that you can't upsell your online customers with your higher-level, higher-priced offerings later. Most of them will be interested in knowing what else you can help them with, especially if they are satisfied with, or even better—loved, the products or services they have already tried.

In fact, you can post discounts and incentives online for all your products that are exclusive to your website in order to drive traffic and increase your page rankings. The excitement of your website combined with the high-quality, high-value products or services you are offering will also keep them from turning to your competitors for business solutions or assistance.

TIP: Set a meeting with your employees or speak with your business coach (www.sharkbitecoaching.com) to decide which products are best introduced and/or sold on your website. These should be the products that are popular, easy to deliver, and caters most specifically to your target market to ensure you get a lot of attention, visitors, and (of course) conversions.

COMMANDMENT #3
YOU SHALL MAKE IT AS EASY AS POSSIBLE FOR A CUSTOMER TO MAKE A PURCHASE

Incorporate a Big 'Buy Now' Button and a Fully-Functional, Reliable Payment Processing System

It is important for you to accept credit card payments from Visa and MasterCard (and even American Express) to encourage first-time users to try your products. There are other all-inclusive programs or plug-ins that automate your sales, payment processing, and delivery in one place. Remember that your website isn't just a method of advertising; it also serves as an extension of your company and you need to give interested customers easy options for ordering your products or services as quickly and efficiently as possible.

A website cannot function as part of a business if customers cannot make purchases through it (The online brochure is out-of-date and will reap no rewards), and this is why you need the right e-commerce tool to allow customers to find, check out, and purchase items. The easiest way to do this is to add shopping cart functionality to your site.

A shopping cart doesn't just serve as an online commercial or virtual catalog; it also helps your customers remain organized. They can easily add and remove items from their 'shopping cart' and browse through the best products, sizes, colors, prices, and any other options you have available.

Aside from making online purchasing easy for your customers, a shopping cart also makes the process of online commerce easier for you by making sure to add shipping fees and if necessary, sales tax, to every purchase. The best shopping carts work with FedEx, UPS, and the other major shipping companies to give your customers fast and reliable service.

Along with the convenience of a shopping cart for your customers, you can have a payment processing system that accepts all major credit cards. The most popular shopping carts are Google CheckOut, Yahoo! Stores, eBay ProStores, ZenCart, 3DCart, and 1ShoppingCart. If you prefer to have your own e-commerce software rather than just an online tool, CS-Cart offers great professional features for your business.

TIP: Any delays or glitches in the functionality of your website or order/payment processing program can quickly lead to lost business, so your shopping cart plug-in or software should be checked on a regular basis. Any problems you encounter should be reported to their administrators or technical support right away so they can fix them as soon as possible. You should also have a back-up plan for taking orders or accepting requests for orders when your order processing service is non-functional. A simple default page with a notice and an email can do the trick. But make sure you promptly follow-up with those customers who emailed you—as with so many online options—they won't bother coming back on their own.

COMMANDMENT #4
IT SHALL BE EASY FOR CUSTOMERS TO CONTACT YOU

Provide all your business contact information and make it easy to find

Nowadays, pretty much anyone can create a website, and to show that you and your business are credible, you must display all possible methods through which people can reach you. Your complete contact information includes your company name, address, phone, email and fax, and all of these must be displayed on your website.

People who visit your site should be able to find where your business is based. Street numbers, towns, cities, phone numbers, fax numbers, and email addresses should all be posted, and if you have a Facebook page and Twitter address for your business, by all means post them as well. Adding your location to your website, not just in the contact information section but in the main page and keywords too, can help people relate more to you and your products and services. They see you as someone real and relatable. You will also earn more local clients using this method since Google Places considers local listings a priority in their rankings and searches connected to your business keywords.

It is an inevitable fact that the more reachable you are, the more successful your business will be. But if someone calls your number, will they get an answering machine?

When launching or growing a business, it's impossible to be everything to everyone and the receptionist role would probably fall pretty low on your "to do/to be" list. There are ways around this, most are actually pretty cost-effective.

Services such as PatLive can take care of the customer calls, order entries, online management, and other jobs that a receptionist normally handles, leaving you free to focus on other business aspects. But if you want to get more bang for your buck, you can hire a virtual assistant (either part-time or full-time) from companies such as VA Networking, Assistant Match, or Elance. You can even find a virtual assistant from popular social media and commerce websites like Craigslist and Twitter!

However, there is also the option of a virtual assistant from the Philippines, which you can check out as http://bit.ly/TFYXDi. Any of these solutions offer you a smart, skilled professional who can also assist with additional tasks. The choice is yours but you may find that one of these options meets your expectations in skills, availability, and cost best. So don't shortchange yourself—do your research and interview potential candidates. Your ideal virtual assistant awaits. You just need to find each other.

TIP: When you register your domain name and set up your hosting account (by the way, this doesn't necessarily have to be with the same company—so shop around for the best options and pricing!) go ahead and set up a few email addresses you know you will need (i.e. info@, help@, privacy@, etc). You can always go back later and do this, but it is more efficient to do it while you are in 'set up' mode.

Make sure you add this, your address, telephone, and fax numbers (if applicable). [You can get an incoming number from Google Voice that forwards to any phone you tell it to if you are just starting out...] This is the first step to easy access for your customers and also makes it a breeze when you decide to engage a virtual assistant (http://bit.ly/TFYXDi) or online management support services (www.social-media-management-group.com).

COMMANDMENT #5
THOU SHALL INTRIGUE YOUR WEBSITE VISITORS WITH AMAZING WRITING AND FRESH IDEAS

Don't underestimate the power of great writing. It's imperative to keeping potential customers on your site.

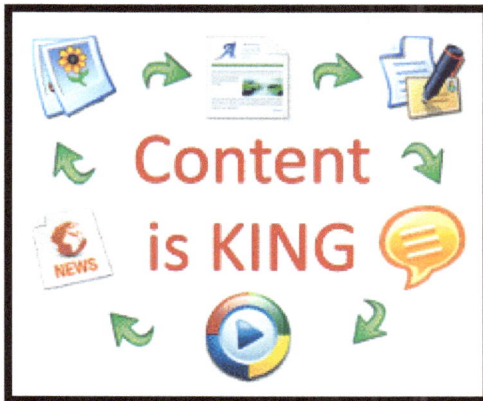

The design and layout of your website may be the first thing that catches the attention of your visitors (potential customers), but it's the content that will retain their interest and keep them on your site. This means that your website needs to be clear, concise, informative, entertaining, and honest.

Explain your products and services clearly, concisely, and in the most interesting way you can imagine.

One common marketing strategy used by popular corporations is to leave a tantalizing or subtle message that will peak the interest of your potential and existing customers. However, these big businesses are already well known. For smaller businesses that are not as well known yet, you need to show people what your products and services are about right from the start (especially what you can do for them, what problem you can solve, what value you can add…), and you can do that with great copywriting. Your potential customers may be left feeling dumb if they don't understand what your advertisement or business is about, and don't assume they will call or email you to get more information, because they probably won't bother.

You need to show your visitors what your product does, how it differs from its competition, and how you can solve their problems—quickly and effectively. Make use of your Unique Selling Proposition (USP) or differentiator to firmly establish what makes your product stand out and to reach as many interested customers as you can.

Use testimonials and client/customer reviews

Praise for your hard work is kudos well-deserved, and you should get as much mileage out of these testimonials as you possibly can by adding them, along with reviews, prominently on your website. Potential clients are more likely to believe what other customers say about you and your products than what you say about you and your products. Hopefully these testimonials and reviews will prove that your products really do work and that your services are worth trying, making you seem reliable and trustworthy.

There are different ways to do this…create a page of testimonials and reviews with a link from your main menu or add a scrolling widget to your home page if you are just getting started and only have a few. Other businesses may scatter their testimonials on their pages…this is yet another example you can follow, but keep them neat and short so they won't distract from the main content of the pages. If you want to include the name and city of the people who gave those reviews, ask their permission first before posting them on your website. In short, use the reviews your products and services received, but never ever make up stories that aren't true or features that your products or services don't have or can't provide.

TIP: If you need some testimonials or reviews…ask for them from your repeat and satisfied customers. But ask permission to use first name, city and possibly an image at the same time you are asking for a testimonial so you don't have to go back later to do it.

Having great reviews and testimonials is excellent, but not being able to attach a name/photo/place to it renders it nearly useless. So know what you need the first time you ask and save time, trouble, and frustration later.

For more assistance in this 'trickier' part of your business, visit www.social-media-management-group.com/ORMR, they are well versed in online reputation management and restoration.

COMMANDMENT #6
THOU SHALL GIVE YOUR WEBSITE VISITOR MOVEMENT AND ACTION

Don't include all of your information on one long page. Create dimension with multiple pages—Link accurately and keep load time short.

There's a reason why the most popular songs nowadays are shorter than five minutes, studies show that the average human gets bored easily with tedious and drawn-out activities. This is why you shouldn't confine your website to a single page that will require the reader to scroll up and down to get the information about your products and services. If your website is difficult to navigate, the customers (or potential customers) visiting your website will get fed up and leave your site without giving you another thought. Not to state the obvious but—this is bad...

It is best to break your site into different pages covering different aspects and products, and create a header menu or side menu for the more active pages; a footer menu can also be added to keep important—but less used—links on every page. (These may include privacy policy, terms and conditions, etc). Use links to keep your website neat, organized, and engaging. A single page should not display all the information about your company, for it will look too messy and unappealing—and scrolling is boring.

Highlight links on your main page that people can click on for specific details about the different products and services you have. The order of links is very important as well as the words you use, which should be relevant to the page that the link connects to. These highlight links can also rotate to enhance the movement of the page and further engage your visitors and potential customers. But don't let this type of functionality slow down the load time of your site or individual pages...in the grand scheme of things, fast loading pages take priority over adding fun features that don't add much value and, often, reduce ease of functionality.

The worst thing you can do is have your main page act like an About Us section and display the entire history, purpose, and goals of your business or worse—your vision, products, story of your life, why you started the business, and the childhood pet you named the company after—well, you get the point. Remember that people will come to your site mainly to learn more about what you are offering and how it can help them solve a problem, so give them what they are looking for. The company name and link to your most popular service or product should be clearly displayed on your homepage for starters.

You should also aim to keep your content fresh. Regularly changing content or adding items of interest (new products, testimonials, reviews, images, case studies, etc.) to your website will not only keep visitors returning, but it helps to elevate your site (or individual pages of your site) in the page rankings for the keywords you have chosen to focus on. (Need assistance with keyword research and selection, visit www.social-media-management-group.com/what-i-do/)

TIP: This is another reason why it is important for you to have a regular update schedule for your website. As your business grows, you can create and change content as required and add additional pages and links for more products. As keywords churn, your copy will also need updating to ensure you are ranking for all relevant keywords and phrases (including long-tail keywords...stumped ya, huh? No problem. Email info@social-media-management-group.com for keyword research assistance).

COMMANDMENT #7
AN ACCOMPLISHED WEBMASTER YOU SHALL BECOME

Make sure you are tracking your website's analytics. This helps with adjusting your marketing methods to drive traffic. Without traffic, there is no reason to have a website and this Book becomes useless.

It's important to spread the word about your website, but it's just as important for you to constantly check on how your promotional efforts are doing. Don't immediately assume that traffic will continue to flow to your website or that it will be a continuous source of new customers without any help from you; you must track just how much of your new business it has brought in from the day it was launched and within certain time frames (like when you are running a sale or certain promotion). It is also important to understand how the traffic ebbs and flows so you can plan traffic boosting promotions during times that it would normally be lower.

This is especially imperative when determining the success or failure of your marketing campaigns, advertisements, and e-mail blasts. From the start, keep track of all the business you gained from it. Keeping a record of your website traffic results (including click through rates, purchases, and other types of conversions) will give you an idea of which products and services are getting the most attention. This should then inform any future marketing efforts to either re-launch slower-moving products or expand marketing on your more successful products to capitalize further. That way, you will know whether your website is working well, and you may even get some ideas on how to make the various aspects of your website even better (more specifically your copywriting and design). Remember that there is always room for improvement and a good website can be made great (if you know where it is lacking or which sections could use some focused enhancements).

TIP: Create a separate section in your marketing plan that details the business you gained and lost from your website based on your conversion rates. This helps you find the best strategies to garner more Internet traffic towards your website. Google Analytics and Webmaster Tools are great tools to help you with this; although many hosting companies have these stats available through certain free programs found on your c-panel. [Not sure what I am talking about, let me explain further by contacting me at info@social-media-management-group.com]

COMMANDMENT #8
THOU SHALL BUILD A WEBSITE TO BE
PROUD OF SO YOUR CUSTOMERS WILL
RETURN AGAIN AND AGAIN

Get the most professional-looking website you can afford…both design and copy should be considered…and incorporate continuity programs.

Websites are like books and magazines. If people don't find it interesting at first glance or on their first visit, they won't care what it's about and will not be returning any time soon. A website should look crafty and be interesting to read and engaging, so make yours as interactive, intriguing, and entertaining as you possibly can. People should want to learn more by clicking on various links throughout your website.

The quickest way to get a professional-looking website is to have a professional web designer build one. The best website designers won't just supply you with a really great site but they also understand all the other meticulous details you may not have thought of or considered, such as a good website name or URL and the most versatile fonts and colors that are globally available and proven to get [and keep] people's interest. [This is an important consideration. Once your website is designed to look a certain way, it is necessary to ensure that it appears to your customer that way. Unfortunately, the way your site appears depends on the software on the viewer's computer. It is almost completely out of your hands as using an obscure font will force your customer's or client's computer to replace that font with a more germane (ugly) one, and it will have a detrimental effect on the entire look and feel of your site—causing it to lose its effectiveness.]

You may know the exact content you want posted on your site, but a good designer will know how to display it in such a layout and format that everyone who visits will be able to easily view your copy and will want to stay to learn more about your company.

If you are well-versed in topics such as domain name registration and website design and development, you may not need to hire a website designer but you should check out the sites of popular businesses to study the look, tone, and functionality of those you think are really good ones.

Continuity programs are those that give your visitors a reason to keep coming back to your site to maintain regular communication with you...regularly scheduled newsletters or expert interviews posted weekly or monthly are just a couple of the methods that are used today. These should be reliable and also incorporated into your overall marketing plan and social media marketing initiatives. Not sure which continuity program you should undertake? Let me help you. Send an email to info@social-media-management-group.com.

Building the best website for your company will take time and money, but it's well spent once business from your online relationships starts to pour in.

TIP: There is a great exercise for you to undertake whether you are designing your site yourself or outsourcing it.

Search the web for websites of companies you know, use, or just like.

1.   *Analyze those sites*

2.   *Take notes on the aspects of those sites that you really love, like, dislike, wish you could do, wish you had a reason to do, know what you will never do, etc.*

3.   *Knowing the various aspects of other sites like this can help direct the designer towards a site that you find pleasing while building in the necessary functionality you believe your visitors would enjoy and appreciate.*

CONCLUSION

I think you are getting the picture now…

A high conversion website is user-friendly, entertaining, and easy to navigate, and more often than not—has a 'simple' (not boring) look and design that is guaranteed to get and keep people's interest while prompting the desired actions (conversions). Having your own company website means that you can help your business move to levels of recognition that would have been difficult, if not impossible to achieve before.

It should also help you in increasing your conversions and the size of your mailing/emailing list. A list of targeted prospects is the gold at the end of this rainbow.

We hope that these commandments and subsequent tips will prove helpful to you now and in the future. Remember, a website should never be static so you can incorporate different tips over time and test out the response.

ABOUT THE AUTHOR

Cassandra Fenyk is a dynamic marketer, speaker, and motivator with extensive experience in various B2B and B2C industries, and unlike many other website and social media consultants, she is also an established marketing professional with nearly 20 years of experience in developing and directing business-to-consumer and business-to-business market penetration strategies. She has spent the majority of her career entrenched in branding, messaging, strategic planning, and project management. She has a keen understanding of the selling process and the critical steps between the initial message, the final sale, and post-sale relationship maintenance. Combined with her knowledge and experience in managing social media and website SEO programs, these traits make her a great source of information and an invaluable resource for your business.

Most recently, Ms. Fenyk started her coaching business focusing on start-ups, small businesses, and entrepreneurs; and all the characteristics that entails. Shark Bite Coaching (www.sharkbitecoaching.com) is that business and if you would like more personalized assistance in avoiding common business pitfalls, overcoming obstacles to your business growth, and getting your business moving in the right direction, ask her and set up an appointment to discuss your ideas and goals.

RECOMMENDED READING LIST

HTML and CSS: Design and Build Websites
Jon Duckett

Python for Data Analysis
Wes McKinney

Learning Web Design: A Beginner's Guide to HTML, CSS, JavaScript, and Web Graphics
Jennifer Niederst Robbins

Don't Make Me Think: A Common Sense Approach to Web Usability, 2nd Edition
Steve Krug

JavaScript: The Good Parts
Douglas Crockford

LOOK FOR MORE BUSINESS-BUILDING AND BUSINESS EXCELLENCE BOOKS BY SHARK BITE COACHING ON AMAZON

Shark Bite Coaching
PO Box 373
Florham Park, NJ 07932
shark@sharkbitecoaching.com

A Note to the Reader:

This manual is intended to give guidance on the different issues and mistakes that are often made with the creation, launch, and maintenance of a corporate website. Consult your attorney, tax accountant, or other professional advisors before choosing the right path for you and your business.

www.sharkbitecoaching.com